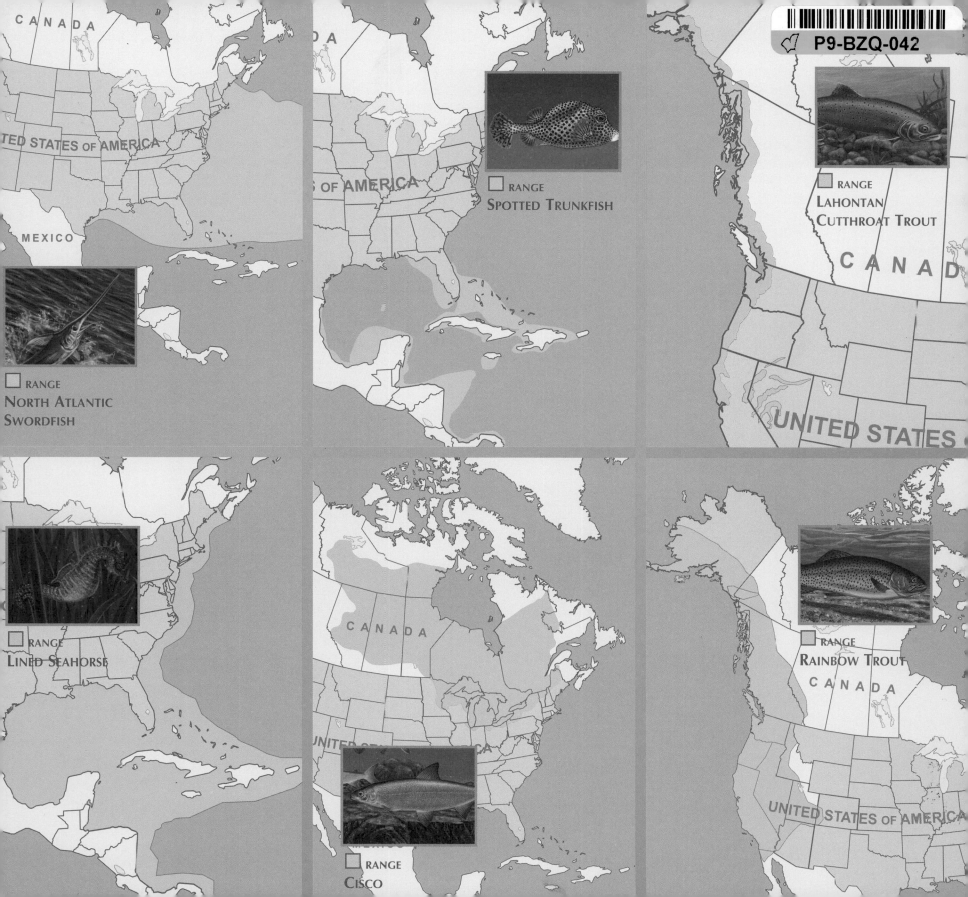

☐ RANGE
SPOTTED TRUNKFISH

☐ RANGE
LAHONTAN
CUTTHROAT TROUT

☐ RANGE
NORTH ATLANTIC
SWORDFISH

☐ RANGE
LINED SEAHORSE

☐ RANGE
CISCO

☐ RANGE
RAINBOW TROUT

A PLACE FOR
FISH

For Doug, who loves to fish
but respects his catch
—M. S.

In memory of my sister, Fareedah Muhammad,
and my father, Henry Drew Higgins, who taught
me about the great places for fish in Arkansas
—H. B.

Ω

Published by
PEACHTREE PUBLISHERS
1700 Chattahoochee Avenue
Atlanta, Georgia 30318-2112
www.peachtree-online.com

Text © 2011, 2018 by Melissa Stewart
Illustrations © 2011, 2018 by Higgins Bond

Edited by Vicky Holifield
Book design by Loraine M. Joyner
Composition by Melanie McMahon Ives

Illustrations created in acrylic on cold press illustration board
Title typeset in Hardlyworthit; main text typeset in Monotype's Century
Schoolbook with Optima initial capitals; sidebars typeset in Optima

Printed and manufactured in Malaysia
10 9 8 7 6 5 4 3 2 1
Revised Edition

HC: 978-1-68263-011-2
PB: 978-1-68263-012-9

Library of Congress Cataloging-in-Publication Data
Stewart, Melissa.
A place for fish / written by Melissa Stewart ; illustrated by Higgins Bond.
  p. cm.
ISBN 978-1-56145-562-1
1. Rare fishes—Juvenile literature. 2. Fishes—Effect of human beings
on—Juvenile literature. 3. Fishes—Ecology—Juvenile literature. I. Bond,
Higgins, ill. II. Title.
  QL617.7.S74 2011
  597.17—dc22
      2010026689

A PLACE FOR
FISH

Written by
Melissa Stewart

Illustrated by
Higgins Bond

Ω
PEACHTREE
ATLANTA

Fish make our world a better place. But sometimes people do things that make it hard for them to live and grow.

If we work together to help these special creatures, there will always be a place for fish.

ON THE MOVE

A fish swims by bending its body from side to side. Its strong tail pushes it forward through the water. Paired fins on its sides help it start, stop, and turn. Top and bottom fins help a fish keep its balance. Fish with slim fins and a narrow tail can swim fast. Fish with large, wide fins and a square tail swim slowly, but they can turn quickly.

masked angelfish

For fish to survive, they need to stay safe and healthy. Some sharks die when they're accidentally hooked by fishing lines.

When fishing crews use hooks that the sharks can detect from a distance, fish can live and grow.

HAMMERHEAD SHARK

Hammerhead sharks have lived on Earth for more than ten million years. But now they're in trouble. Each year, thousands of these sharks die when they get caught on fishing lines set out for tuna and swordfish. Recently, scientists discovered that hammerheads can sense some kinds of metal fishing hooks. When fishing crews use these hooks, hammerheads know that they should stay away.

Some fish are harmed by the chemicals power plants produce when they burn coal to make electricity.

NORTHERN PIKE

As power plants burn coal to make electricity, they pump out smoke full of chemicals. The chemicals mix with clouds to produce acid rain. When the acid rain comes into contact with rocks at the bottom of a lake, the rocks release a material that damages fish gills. How can we help save northern pikes and other fish? By conserving electricity and using solar power and wind power in more homes and businesses.

a wind farm

When people find other ways to make electricity, fish can live and grow.

Some fish are so beautiful that people like to keep them as pets.

YELLOW TANG

Each year, divers collect as many as five hundred thousand yellow tangs from Hawaii's coral reefs. They know that people with home aquariums will pay a lot of money for the colorful fish. But now the number of yellow tangs in the ocean is falling.

In 2015, scientists learned how to breed yellow tangs in their labs. If people buy these fish instead of wild ones, yellow tangs can make a comeback.

yellow tang

When people stop catching these colorful creatures, fish can live and grow.

Some fish have unusual body parts that people like to collect.

When laws stop people from selling the special body parts, fish can live and grow.

SMALLTOOTH SAWFISH

For centuries, healers in Asia added sawfish fins to their remedies. They thought the fins had magical powers. People in other parts of the world collected the fish's long, toothy snout. By the 1990s, there were almost no sawfish left.

In 2014, the smalltooth sawfish was added to the U.S. Endangered Species List. Now it's against the law to sell any part of a sawfish. The fish is still in danger, but scientists hope it will be able to survive.

Some fish can't survive when people add new kinds of fish to rivers, streams, lakes, and ponds.

SMALLMOUTH BASS

Many people buy young goldfish as pets. But when the fish outgrow their tank, their owners may decide to dump them in a local pond. Goldfish eat smaller native fish such as smallmouth bass and their eggs. And as goldfish feed, they destroy bass nests by stirring up mud and sand. People should never release a goldfish in a natural body of water.

smallmouth bass

When people stop dumping pet goldfish into local waters,
native fish can live and grow.

Some fish taste so delicious that people catch and eat too many of them.

NORTH ATLANTIC SWORDFISH

At one time, millions of swordfish lived along the Atlantic coast of North America. But by the 1990s, they were in danger of disappearing forever. Chefs across North America took swordfish off their menus. Then the U.S. Congress banned fishing in areas where swordfish lay their eggs. Soon, the problem was solved. Today there are plenty of swordfish swimming in the sea.

When scientists, chefs, and lawmakers work together,
fish can live and grow.

Fish also have trouble surviving when their natural homes are destroyed. Some fish can only live near coral reefs.

When people work to protect coral reefs, fish can live and grow.

SPOTTED TRUNKFISH

The spotted trunkfish depends on Florida's coral reefs for food and shelter. But these reefs face many dangers. Chemicals in household cleaners make coral animals weak, so they can't fight diseases. Boats bump into reefs and destroy them. To help solve the problem, volunteer groups like Reef Environmental Education Foundation (REEF) are teaching people ways to protect coral reefs and the fish that call them home.

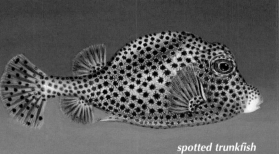

spotted trunkfish

Sometimes ranchers drain water from lakes and streams, so their animals will have enough to drink. But that can make it hard for fish to survive.

LAHONTAN CUTTHROAT TROUT

In the western United States, many ranchers get water for their cattle from nearby lakes and streams. The shallow water warms up quickly in the sun. Then it evaporates, leaving behind salt. The warm, salty water isn't a good home for Lahontan cutthroat trout.

Luckily, groups like Trout Unlimited are working with ranchers to conserve water. Programs like this may help the fish make a comeback.

When people find ways to use less water, fish can live and grow.

Some ocean habitats are destroyed when people use chemicals to make their lawns thick and green.

When people stop using these chemicals, fish can live and grow.

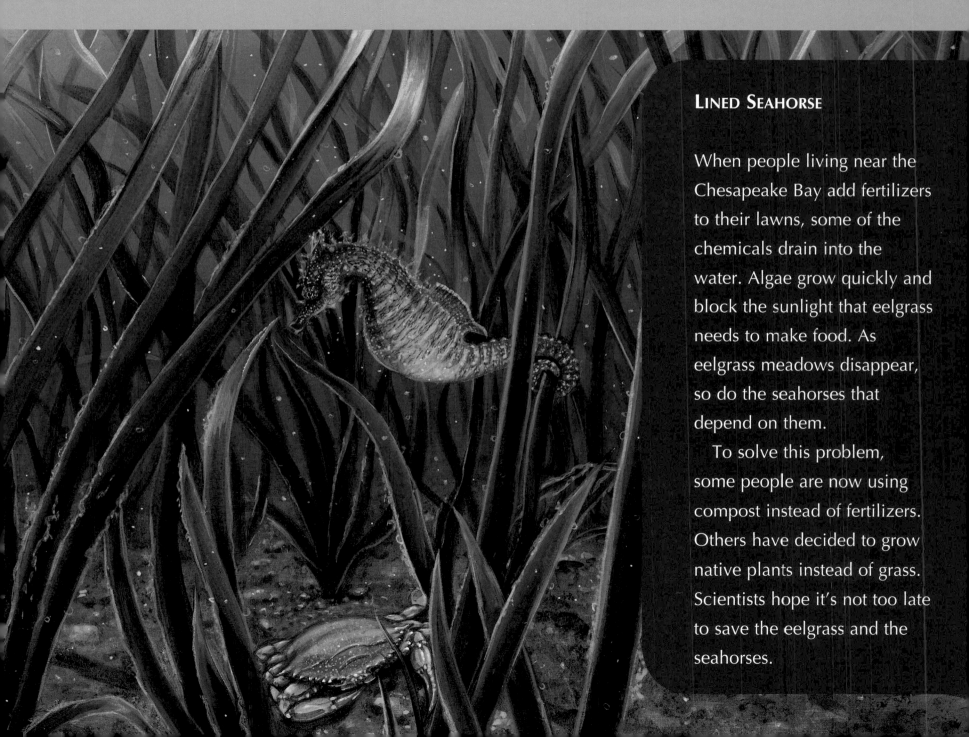

LINED SEAHORSE

When people living near the Chesapeake Bay add fertilizers to their lawns, some of the chemicals drain into the water. Algae grow quickly and block the sunlight that eelgrass needs to make food. As eelgrass meadows disappear, so do the seahorses that depend on them.

To solve this problem, some people are now using compost instead of fertilizers. Others have decided to grow native plants instead of grass. Scientists hope it's not too late to save the eelgrass and the seahorses.

Some fish can only survive in deep, cold lake water. As climate change caused by the use of fossil fuels heats our planet, these fish are dying.

When people use less oil, coal, and natural gas to heat their homes and power their cars, fish can live and grow.

Cisco

In recent summers, thousands of cisco and other fish have been dying in Minnesota's lakes. What's to blame? Hot weather caused by burning fossil fuels for energy.

When lake water heats up, cisco are trapped. They can't swim to cooler waters. And since cisco are an important source of food for bigger fish, the heat is bad news for those fish too. What's the solution to this problem? Using less energy. If we can slow global warming soon, we may be able to save cisco and other lake fish.

We build dams to control the flow of water along rivers and streams. But the dams make it hard for fish to swim from place to place.

RAINBOW TROUT

In 1921, workers built the Savage Rapids Dam across the Rogue River in Oregon. The dam made it hard for rainbow trout and salmon to swim upstream and lay their eggs. It also blocked young fish from swimming downstream. In 2009, workers tore down the dam. According to scientists, letting the river flow free is saving more than one hundred thousand fish every year.

rainbow trout

When people remove dams, fish can live and grow.

W hen too many fish die, other living things may also struggle to survive.

WE NEED FISH

Fish help us survive. People living in the United States eat about eight billion pounds of fish every year. Fish is an important source of protein. It also keeps our hearts healthy and improves memory. Most experts say people should eat fish at least three times a week.

That's why it's so important to protect fish and the places where they live.

OTHER ANIMALS NEED FISH

Fish are an important part of the food chain. Fish eggs are good sources of food for turtles and for other fish. Adult fish are eaten by bears, raccoons, muskrats, otters, seals, bats, and birds. Without fish, many other creatures would go hungry.

F ish have lived on Earth for more than 450 million years. Sometimes people do things that can harm fish.

But there are many ways you can help these special creatures live far into the future.

HELPING FISH

❖ If you catch a small fish, let it go.

❖ Always wash fishing gear thoroughly before using it in another body of water. This will help prevent invasive species from spreading.

❖ Do not throw trash into any body of water.

❖ Do not pour household cleaners or other chemicals down the drain.

❖ Conserve water. Don't let it run while you brush your teeth. Take showers instead of baths. Collect rainwater and use it to water plants.

❖ Join a group of people working to protect or restore rivers, lakes, streams, ponds, or ocean areas near your home.

FISH FACTS

* No one knows how many kinds of fish live on Earth. So far, scientists have discovered more than twenty-five thousand different species. Some researchers think there may fifteen thousand more species left to identify.

* Most fish swim in groups called schools, but a group of seahorses is called a herd.

* The stout infantfish is the smallest fish on Earth. It could easily sit on top of a pencil eraser. The great whale shark is the world's largest fish. It's bigger than a school bus.

* Fish don't have eyelids, so they can't close their eyes and fall asleep like we do. Most fish rest quietly at night, but some fish are almost always on the move.

* Most young fish are called fingerlings, but young sharks and sawfish are called pups.

SELECTED SOURCES

Adams, Jake. "Yellow Tangs Finally Captive Bred by the Oceanic Institute." *Reef Builders,* October 20, 2015. Available online at *www.reefbuilders. com/2015/10/20/yellow-tangs-finally-captive-bred-oceanic-institute*

Burr, Brooks M. and Lawrence M. Page. *A Field Guide to Freshwater Fishes: North America North of Mexico.* Boston: Houghton Mifflin, 1991.

"Final Endangered Listing of Five Species of Sawfish Under the Endangered Species Act." *Federal Registar: The Daily Journal of the United States Government,* December 12, 2014. Available online at *www.federalregister.gov/documents/2014/12/12/2014-29201/endangered-and-threatened-wildlife-and-plants-final-endangered-listing-of-five-species-of-sawfish*

"Hammerhead Sharks' Unique Traits May Doom Them." *Conservation,* June 25, 2014. Available online at *www.conservationmagazine.org/2014/06/hammerhead-sharks-unique-traits-may-doom-them*

National Audubon Society. *Field Guide to North American Fishes.* New York: Knopf, 2002.

Pelton, Tom. "Rare and Romantic Seahorses Threatened by Pollution and Fishing." *Bay Daily,* October 25, 2012. Available online at *www.cbf.typepad.com/bay_daily/2012/10/rare-and-romantic-seahorses-threatened-by-pollution-and-fishing.html*

"Savage Rapids Dam Removal." *Waterwatch of Oregon.* Available online at *www.waterwatch.org/programs/savage-rapids-dam-removal*

Schultz, Ken. *Field Guide to Saltwater Fish.* New York: Wiley, 2003.

"Will Lake Warming in Minnesota Drive Cold-water Fish to Extinction?" St. Anthony Falls Laboratory, University of Minnesota. Available online at *www.safl.umn. edu/featured-story/will-lake-warming-minnesota-drive-cold-water-fish-extinction*

RECOMMENDED FOR YOUNG READERS

Fish: *http://animals.nationalgeographic.com/animals/fish*

Fish Videos: *http://www.kidport.com/reflib/science/Videos/Animals/Fish/FishVideoIndex.htm#Menu*

Parker, Steve. *Fish.* New York: Knopf, 2005.

Sayre, April Pulley. *Trout Are Made of Trees.* Watertown, MA: Charlesbridge, 2008.

Secrets of the Seahorse: *http://aquarium.ucsd.edu/Education/Learning_Resources/Secrets_of_the_Seahorse*

ACKNOWLEDGMENTS

The author wishes to thank Doug Stewart, Wetland Scientist and Senior Principal, Stantec Consulting, for his help in preparing this manuscript.